SECONDARY SCHOOL ADMINISTRATION SERIES

David B. Austin, Editor

Schools Within Schools

A STUDY OF

HIGH SCHOOL ORGANIZATION

KARL R. PLATH

Bureau of Publications 1965

Teachers College, Columbia University, New York

Editor's Introduction

LEARNING IS A VERY PERSONAL BUSINESS. EDUCATION, IN ITS MORE formal setting, is public business and big business. The obvious difficulties of reconciling the purpose to be accomplished by the creation of schools with the essence of the learning process, and all of its complexities, demands the thoughtful attention of all who make decisions about the organization of school systems and, in particular, of schools themselves.

The history of American programs for youth education does not clearly record the bases upon which such decisions have been made in the past. However, it is safe to assume that until very recently the deployment of persons and space was a matter left to chance and simple convenience rather than to studied planning. Much of what developed, fortunately, seemed to work fairly well in a setting that allowed for few students and few teachers assembled for clear and specific purposes. Those who succeeded and survived did have the personal attention of teachers to a remarkable extent, and the school—in particular the high school—was effective to the degree to which the individual teacher recognized individual learners as warm, human beings. In a close, small setting within a clearly identifiable community this is not difficult to accomplish.

Yesterday's schools were for yesterday, and tomorrow's schools are to be for a future that includes a maze of unknowns. Yet it seems quite clear that urbanization, improved means of transportation, and rapidly expanded demands on the secondary school will force larger and larger complexes devoted to the education of young people. Indeed, such complexes do exist today and are growing month by month in their complexity. These are unusual institutions whose characteristics and problems are notable for their rate of change and their difficult demands on management and organization. Yet where these large schools are the exception today, they will most likely be common tomorrow.

The planning for such complexes can no longer be left to simple chance nor to common convenience. Rather, it must be based upon the best that can be developed in a disciplined and rational sense. Theory, reenforced by increasing studied experience, is needed if the internal organization of such enterprises is to enhance rather than jeopardize the opportunity for individuals to learn to behave as rational human integers in the setting of mass treatment.

Dr. Plath has made a tentative but significant step in this study of a very promising approach to the large high school and its internal organization. He is particularly qualified to deal with such a topic, having observed one such school over a period of years from within as a teacher and administrator, and he is currently the chief administrative officer of another school system within which many of the very problems with which this volume deals must shortly be solved. Although there is a tentative quality to this report, it deals with experience, both successful and otherwise, hammered out by competent and imaginative educators. Here is a systematic documentation of that effort. It is worthy of the thoughtful attention of all persons concerned with the education of American youth today—particularly in anticipation of tomorrow's demands.

DAVID B. AUSTIN
Professor of Education
Teachers College, Columbia University

Contents

Schools Within Schools

A STUDY OF
HIGH SCHOOL ORGANIZATION

Introduction

The status of the individual must remain our primary concern. All our institutions—political, social, and economic—must further enhance the dignity of the citizen, promote the maximum development of his capabilities, stimulate their responsible exercise, and widen the range and effectiveness of opportunities for individual choice (1:2).*

This monograph discusses a plan of school organization that emphasizes the individual student. Schools-within-a-school organization works daily in an increasing number of United States secondary schools. Definition and description of this method of organization, its development, examples of its use, its unique physical facilities, its personnel needs, and suggestions for its use are detailed on following pages.

A DEFINITION

What are schools within a school? Those claiming to use this organization would give varying answers. For our purpose, because of the broad range of examples to be covered, the following definition seems most acceptable: The schools-within-a-school plan is an organizational design whereby a large secondary school is divided into smaller schools. Each little school has its

* Numbers in parentheses refer to items in the bibliography on pages 81–83. Specific page numbers follow the reference number when an author is quoted directly.

own administrative leadership, guidance staff, and students. Each little school has building spaces assigned to its exclusive use. A part of each student's school day is spent within the building area of his little school. Although faculty members may be assigned to each little school, a student's curricular class activities are provided both by this group and by faculty shared among the several little schools.

Houses, divisions, little schools, units—such terms are used in practice to describe subdivisions in the decentralized organization defined above. In this monograph, because of personal preference and for brevity, we will use little schools and units as synonyms for schools within the school.

A DILEMMA

Two trends of the past decade challenge the thinking about secondary school organization for the 1960's. Schools have grown dramatically in size; and concurrently there has persisted a concern for the individual student as secondary institutions become larger.

Growth in size of secondary schools

Pressures of enrollment have placed increasing burdens on numerous American secondary schools. The United States Office of Education documented this in a study which showed that an increasing percentage of schools have enrollments of at least 200 students. The median high school enrollment grew from 175 to 278 between 1952 and 1959. This growth pattern indicates important gains in the "typical" high school's size. Of special significance is the fact that although only about 5 per cent of the secondary schools enroll 1500 or more pupils, 22 per cent of the nation's secondary school enrollment is in such schools (33).

One cause of larger schools has been the reduction in number of public school districts. And this trend will continue. Even

2

though the total number of districts has already been cut substantially (from 94,926 in 1947–48 to 63,057 in 1953–54; 47,594 in 1957–58; and 31,319 in 1963–64), many states are introducing legislation that will shrink the number still further. Since the President's Commission On National Goals has set 10,000 districts as an ideal maximum number, further reduction seems likely (1).

The support of educational authorities has also speeded the trend to larger secondary schools. Conant has named district reorganization, with its resulting larger schools, as the prime need in many states if they are to have schools with an adequate curriculum and staff (10). Similarly, a midwestern scholar believes that while finance usually appears as the most important determinant of school quality, size of pupil population follows closely (25).

Another cause of larger secondary schools is, of course, the rise in total pupil population. Projections of future numbers of pupils are startling. For example, the "Rockefeller Report" noted that by 1969 high schools will be deluged with 50 to 70 per cent more students than they could accommodate in 1958 (1).

Concern for the individual

As the forces of larger districts and school populations have combined to produce larger secondary schools, factors in society and in the school situation have joined to increase teacher-administrator concern for individuals. Expansion of public and private education, debates over the quality of mass public education, the increasing use and impact of educational media that encourage mass instruction, and the availability of federal funds for improvement of schools are among the influences that have increased consideration of the individual (22).

Most educators are pleased with this trend; they believe that the school should center on the student, that it should be planned for the students, and that boys and girls need to feel they belong (2, 30). Professional literature, however, has expressed concern

3

that organization in education still lacks the individual point of view. A major project has been initiated by five leading education groups to examine the importance of the individual in the schools of the United States and to consider the implications of individual differences for educational organization and administration and for curriculum content and materials. The first statement issued from this project warns of school practices that reduce the individual's role and therefore oppose the thinking of our nation's founding fathers:

> With an eye to masses rather to than to individuals, the schools are departing from their unique historic character by manipulating pupils and teachers into organizational patterns and by leaning on administrative and mechanical devices that tend to destroy the very quality which has made them great (3:3).

The relationship between concern for the individual and pupil interest in civic-social affairs has been drawn elsewhere. In discussing the individual pupil in the large high school, McNassor has expressed concern about the anonymity of an adolescent in a school of 2000 pupils:

> There may be a direct connection between the apathy of students concerned regarding civic-social matters in the adult community, local, national, and international, and the fact that their time is spent in dense population centers in large high schools which promote feelings of anonymity (26:316).

A PROPOSED SOLUTION

Seeking to solve the dilemma of educating more pupils in larger institutions and providing better individual attention, educators have increasingly turned to the schools-within-a-school plan. The ASCD publication *The Junior High School We Need* states:

> In a junior high school of larger than 500, administrative devices which provide for smaller subunits or for "schools within the school"

are wise. The young adolescent needs to find a respected place for himself. He needs to be known and seen; he deserves attention (19:13).

Proponents of the plan feel that it can produce a broad program of high quality combined with the atmosphere and friendliness of a small school. Through schools within a school the student may retain his individual identity in large groups. Indeed, the AASA School Building Commission report, stressing the need for every high school student to be recognized as an individual, presented the little school as the emotional home base of each of its students—the place where the student receives individual recognition and has contact with someone skilled in guidance (4).

In considering organization to give the needs of individuals proper attention in larger high schools, and realizing that better organization will hasten improved education, the principal and his staff may wish to use the little-school plan. To assure each pupil personal attention of a high quality, this plan of internal organization deserves careful study. Practices at other schools may be applicable. The following pages report common practices in little-school organization with the hope of assisting schools using or considering use of the plan. Dewey once wrote, "A working model is not something to be copied; it is to afford a demonstration of the feasibility of the principle, and of the methods which make it feasible" (13:90). Chapter 2 will begin our discussion of principles and methods of little-school organization by describing the development of the plan.

Development of
Schools Within Schools

WE INTEND TO PRESENT LITTLE-SCHOOL ORGANIZATION AS A MEANS of providing improved individual attention for increasing numbers of secondary school pupils. Since schools using this plan root their organization in principles common to other secondary schools, this chapter will review foundations of secondary school organization before tracing the development of schools within a school.

FOUNDATION IN SECONDARY SCHOOL ORGANIZATION

Organization relates to purpose

Authorities in school administration agree that a close relationship should exist between the organization and the purposes of a school. Effective organization helps a school to achieve its purposes. While the purposes may vary with the communities in which the schools exist, organization is a way to achieve them. What then are the purposes or goals of secondary education?

Goals of secondary education

In a recent yearbook about the American high school, there

7

is a succinct review of the goals of secondary education. The writers' emphatic conclusions, after analyzing statements prominent in clarifying the goals, listed the following goals:

The maximum development of all the mental, moral, emotional, and physical powers of the individual, to the end that he may enjoy a rich life thru the realization of worthy and desirable personal goals.

The maximum development of the ability and desire in each individual to make the greatest possible contribution to all humanity thru responsible participation in, and benefit from, the great privileges of American citizenship (2:28).

Typical school organization

As they design an organization to achieve the above purposes, the principal and staff have the benefit of fresh research. New knowledge about organization, however, has had minor effect on the structural organization of schools. The concept of the "line" function of authority or command and the "staff" function of advice or counsel has continued to dominate the thinking about organization.

Subject-matter departments have traditionally been one of the common components of line and staff organization in the individual secondary school. This departmentalization has been a continuing concern as schools have enlarged their curricula and services. To provide for the coordinated activity of teachers in a subject field through departmentalization, while having the department chairmen and the teachers retain an active interest in other subjects, has been a constant test of the resourcefulness of school administrators.

As faculties have realized the value of lessening departmental loyalties and building added support for the purposes of the entire school, traditional school organization has changed. The use of small conference groups during nonteaching periods, preschool and in-school work conferences, interdepartmental committees, the assignment of teachers to more than one subject, and the teaming of teachers with one group of students are

8

means of lessening the isolation among subject departments (2). As we will see later, little schools may help to solve the same problem. Schools have also been organized without department chairmen. These institutions intend to improve subject coordination through teaching by teams.

Theory in school organization

During the last decade, writers in professional education have shown increasing interest in the development of theory in educational administration. Once lagging in the theoretical sense, educational administration now has moved forward in searching for a theoretical basis for activities.

Emerging from the study of theory is the realization that line and staff organization is not of necessity outmoded or undemocratic. Morphet and others believe that any fault lies not with line and staff structure but in the way the structure is used and in the attitudes of people in the organization (28, 42).

Griffiths' writings have been prominent in literature about theory in educational administration. In a book which summarizes his beliefs, he proposes decision-making as the central process of administration. Matters such as the amount of centralization to have in an organization, Griffiths feels, should be determined by the degree of delegation of authority desired in the decision-making process. In acknowledging the importance of organization, he concludes:

The decision process is an organization matter, and the criterion by which an organization may be evaluated is the quality of the decisions which the organization makes plus the efficiency with which the organization puts the decisions into effect (20:113).

Accepted principles of organization

As their attention to school organization has increased, writers in educational administration have affirmed the importance of evaluation of a school's organization. Since this monograph proposes to study the schools-within-a-school plan as a method of

9

school organization, the plan's structure, as it now operates in schools, will be compared in Chapter 4 with a set of principles commonly accepted in educational administration. The principles are given below.

Of eighteen principles listed by Morphet, the writer has selected twelve as relevant to the focus of this monograph. Other lists of principles might have been chosen. However, the principles indicated are most appropriate because of (a) the emphasis on organization, (b) the recent date of publication, and (c) the recognized position of the authors in the profession.

Principle 1: Organization Structure
    An organizational structure is necessary when any group has a common task.
Principle 2: Unity of Purpose
    The purposes and objectives of an organization must be determined and understood.
Principle 3: Division of Work
    The scheme of organization should provide for maximum homogeneity in the major divisions of work.
Principle 4: Coordination
    Coordination of functions, activities, interests, and assignments is necessary for successful accomplishment of results.
Principle 5: Single Executive
    Every organization should have a single executive head.
Principle 6: Span of Control
    One executive can only deal effectively with a limited number of persons.
Principle 7: Authority and Responsibility
    The necessary authority to accomplish a task should be delegated at the same time that the responsibility for the task is assigned; every person in the organization should know to whom and for what he is responsible, and no individual in the organization should be required to take direct orders from more than one person.
Principle 8: Planning and Decision-Making
    Every organization must make provision for effective planning and decision-making.
Principle 9: Flexibility
    Policies and programs should be stated in terms broad enough to permit reasonable flexibility in management.

Principle 10: Stability
  Continuity of policy and program until results can be evaluated is a prerequisite to good management.
Principle 11: Production
  An effective organization must attain its goals if it is to survive.
Principle 12: Evaluation
  Evaluation is essential to the progress of any group (28:54–61).

DEVELOPMENT BEFORE 1950

Pioneers in little-school organization are schools of different sizes and types in several parts of the country. Information about initiating the plan in these schools follows in chronological sequence.

Cleburne, Texas, High School

Houses were instituted at Cleburne in 1919, after investigation of various educational systems and study of Henry Ford's efforts to make good American citizens of the immigrant workers employed in his Detroit plants. The six little schools, named from a list of famous Americans, were designed to use smaller homeroom groups to create a sense of loyalty and a greater feeling of belonging, to provide more counseling for all, to increase control of discipline cases, and to avoid the administrative confusion inherent in many homeroom situations.

Evanston, Illinois, Township High School

Included in the buildings opened in 1924 were six study halls, each capable of seating 250 students. There was a study hall for each five classrooms, and each study hall was under the guidance of a group supervisor whose office adjoined the study hall. These buildings with their organization of homerooms-study halls were the beginning of schools within schools at Evanston High School. The purpose of the little schools was to provide an education for each pupil within a small-school atmosphere while gaining the advantages of diversity and specialization possible only in a large high school.

11

Brookline, Massachusetts, High School

Initiated in 1934 with 1600 students divided among four units, the unit plan created was similar to a plan in use at Harvard College. The need for decentralization arose when the headmaster (principal) at Brookline realized that he was unable to recognize and know all of the students. Since the school always subscribed to a policy of individual attention, the organization was changed.

Woodrow Wilson Junior High School, Tulsa, Oklahoma

The little-school idea was put into effect here partially in 1937, and fully by 1939. Previously the faculty had acted to improve the integrating and continuity of its subject matter. A key part of the plan was faculty conference groups. In these groups, the teachers assigned to a given number of students would meet within a period in the school day to discuss classroom procedure, pupil-teacher planning, evaluation instruments, and problems of guidance.

William A. Bass High School, Atlanta, Georgia

While the school in Tulsa was developing its little-school organization, a junior high school in Georgia was organizing along similar lines. The Bass Junior High School started the little-school plan in 1938.

At Bass, the pupils were organized into nine units enrolling 160 students each, in order to provide the advantages offered both by small-school situations and by large-school resources.

Although the little-school plan was created for Bass Junior High School, it was found to be easily adaptable when the school was converted to a five-year senior high school in 1947. All of the important features of the plan were preserved when the conversion was made. Since Bass High School had fewer students, the number of little schools was reduced from nine to five—one for each of the five grades, with an enrollment of about 200 in each.

12

Beacon High School, Beacon, New York

Another school developing in the late 1930's was significant in that it contained the first general education laboratory, as planned by N. L. Engelhardt. In Beacon High School, the general education laboratory was a facility within each little school that could accommodate many types of student learning activities. Consisting of a large room surrounded by conference rooms and guidance offices, the general education laboratory could be used for individual work or group work by large or small groups.

Forest Hills High School, New York City

This was the first school to organize large schools within a school. An institution of 3300 students, it opened in 1941 organized as three units of more than 1000 students each.

Focusing on the primary importance of the individual in our educational system, the staff at Forest Hills developed their little-school organization in order to (a) provide the advantages of the smaller school with the flexibility of the large, (b) have a way for the school to know, to guide, and to inspire each pupil, and (c) enable the heads of schools and the guidance counselors to know the problems of each student.

The Pennsbury High School, Fallsington, Pennsylvania

The officials at Pennsbury, realizing in 1948 that there were advantages in personal relationships for the students in their 400-pupil high school, were determined to retain the essence of the smaller school in their future secondary school organization. They therefore began the development of the "2-2-2" organization. The Pennsbury High School now consists of four secondary schools housing two or more grades each: 7–8, 7–10, 9–10, 11–12. No building has been built to exceed 1000-pupil capacity, pupils have been assigned to buildings according to grade, and the grades within each building have been divided into grade-level groups.

13

DEVELOPMENT AFTER 1950

Concurrent with the increasing enrollment and need for added secondary school construction since 1950 has been heightened interest in the schools-within-a-school plan. The impetus of more pupils has encouraged study of school organization, school program, and school design in many communities across the country. Such study has provoked discussion about optimum size of secondary schools. It has also aroused concern about creating a high school too large and too impersonal. In many communities, therefore, the development of schools within a school has been simultaneous with and related to planning a new high school.

A number of school districts were introduced to little-school organization through the efforts of Engelhardt, Engelhardt, and Leggett, an educational consulting firm. This company has continued to develop ideas for the general education laboratory and other aspects of little schools, as first conceived by Nickolaus Engelhardt at Beacon High School in 1938.

A major contribution to the literature about schools within schools was provided in 1958 in the doctoral projects of two students at Teachers College, Columbia University. Selected findings of these projects have implications for school organization and are summarized below.

The Hodgson Study

In summarizing his study of schools within a school, Hodgson listed three advantages that resulted from placing certain administrative duties closer to those immediately affected: (a) there is more effective handling of situations causing control problems, because of the administrator's knowledge of pupils, parents, and home backgrounds; (b) the principal is relieved of routine administrative duties and freed for true educational leadership; and (c) there is increased use of the teachers in policy making.

14

Hodgson reported that the most promising organizational pattern for the little-school plan would seem to be one in which there were an administrator and a guidance counselor in each unit. He urged that clerical assistance be provided for these staff members.

An important problem to consider, according to Hodgson, is the relationship between the subject-matter departments and the little-school organization. Recognizing the need for both vertical coordination of the curriculum within a department and horizontal curriculum integration among departments, Hodgson found no one pattern of organization most satisfactory in the schools studied. However, he stressed the importance of coordination:

. . . there is a need for close coordination of the departments and the little schools to avoid duplication of effort, to insure communication of ideas and practices, and to fix responsibilities for various phases of curriculum development (23:186).

A major strength of schools within schools, as found by Hodgson, was the improvement of the guidance program. Little-school organization enabled teachers to become involved in guidance to a greater extent. In addition, when one or more counselors were assigned to each little-school staff, continuous guidance was emphasized. Also, behavior problems were recognized more quickly in the smaller groups.

In the organization of student activities, Hodgson determined that decentralization of activities on a little-school basis increased participation and added more opportunities for pupils to experience active membership and leadership roles.

The York Study

York's study was limited to a detailed examination and description of four selected secondary schools organized on the schools within a school plan, all housed in buildings designed to house the plan, and all in operation during the 1957–58 school year. Enrollments in the schools studied ranged from 875 to 1400 pupils.

The following are York's generalizations about staff organizational patterns:

Generalization number one. The proper ratio of little school autonomy to school-wide coordination is being sought in all of the schools included in this study. Administrative leadership is provided at the little school unit level in all instances but there is substantial variation in the amount of autonomy afforded the little school unit.

Generalization number two. Subject field coordination is an acknowledged need in all of the schools included in this study. The approaches to the attainment of this coordination, however, are different. There are department chairmen in only one of the four schools (43:121).

York generalized in this way about pupil organization in schools within schools:

Generalization number one. . . . It is the conclusion of the study, based on these four schools, that the problems which arise from the inequitable distribution of pupils among the grade levels require careful evaluation before the grade level plan of pupil assignment is adopted. These problems appear to be particularly acute in schools serving communities with a rapidly increasing population.

Generalization number two. The schools within a school plan can facilitate an increased numerical participation in the pupil activities program. The program must be evaluated also, however, from the point of view of the extent to which pupil identification should be with the little school unit and the extent to which it should be with the school in total (43:123).

PRESENT STATE OF DEVELOPMENT

The use of schools within a school is not exclusive with our country's educational institutions. England has developed campus-type high schools divided into four or five smaller "houses" each serving 150 boys and 150 girls (14).

As did the pioneers in little-school organization, institutions recently beginning the plan have focused on the individual student and studied how decentralization could be used to gain the advantages of small schools as well as of large schools. An excerpt

16

from the educational specifications for the Newton South High School may be considered representative:

Every boy and girl must be thought of as an individual with unique problems, interests, and potentials and not as another face in the crowd. Opportunities for individual expression on the part of the student should be encouraged (9:19).

Although there is no official listing of schools using little-school organization, several sources of information are available. Dr. Stanton Leggett, an educational consultant whose firm has been mentioned previously, estimated in 1960 that fifty schools around the nation had adopted some form of decentralization in the previous five years (32).

In 1960 staff members of the College of Education at Michigan State University conducted a major research study concerning schools within a school. After originally visiting 300 selected secondary schools, the final stage of their project concentrated on thirty selected schools.

The appendix (see pages 77–79) lists the names and locations of schools identified to this writer as using little-school organization. Specific reasons reported for organizing schools within schools have been the following: (a) to create a sense of loyalty and a greater feeling of belonging; (b) to provide more counseling for all students; (c) to have a way for the school to know, guide, and inspire each student; (d) to provide the advantages of small schools with the flexibility and resources of large schools; (e) to improve integration and continuity of subject matter; (f) to increase control of discipline cases; and (g) to avoid the administrative confusion inherent in many homeroom situations.

Chapter 3 will describe in detail how schools within schools are organized to gain the advantages they seek.

Organization of
Schools Within Schools

THE ORGANIZATION DESIGNED BY A PRINCIPAL AND STAFF WILL VARY with their judgments about purposes the organization should accomplish. While there are two common methods of establishing little schools, communities may adopt parts of each to fit their needs. Several fundamental questions must be answered before organizational structure is established and job responsibilities assigned.

PURPOSE—WHY DECENTRALIZE?

Previously we have indicated that the central purpose for forming small schools within a larger institution is to provide better attention to the individual pupil. Faculties desire to maintain a larger school's broad curriculum and specialized facilities while preserving the personal relationships of smaller schools. For example, a Roanoke, Virginia, brochure for staff and community emphasizes little schools' accent on individual pupils by listing their aims as follows:

Improve academic standards and opportunities
Nuture special abilities, talents, and skills
Develop leadership through the multiple activities of the three little
    schools

19

Increase group loyalty and consideration for others among students

Vary classroom procedures and materials through special facilities and equipment

Instill habits of responsibility, cooperation, initiative, promptness, honesty, courtesy, and good health through closer personal attention to each student

Direct student progress through closer faculty and guidance observations and consultations

Utilize the potential of every child to his best advantage

Achieve closer cooperation among faculty, counselors, administration, and parents through the advantage of smaller groups

Lessen drop-outs through individualized programs and continuous progress evaluation (38:4).

Although normally the decision to decentralize results from staff and board of education study of growth projections, or from evaluation that accompanies planning of new facilities, more dramatic evidence may speed the decision. In one school enrolling more than 2000 pupils a senior boy was killed at a nonschool party. When police requested personal information about him from school officials, no faculty member was well acquainted with the boy. This led to a revision of guidance responsibilities as part of decentralization of administrative and guidance services.

The faculty of another school, nearing 3000 pupils in enrollment, was distressed about the number of persistent problems of pupil behavior that had been developing. Pupils involved in such cases were subject to long-term suspension or expulsion. In the year prior to decentralization, 120 such cases were handled. The faculty felt that the school's size and the supervision of student control by a few administrators, who could not know the students, contributed to the amount of misbehavior. For these and other reasons they formed little schools, placing student control among administrators within each unit. During that year only nine major cases arose, despite an enrollment increase.

PUPIL ORGANIZATION—HOW SHOULD PUPILS BE DIVIDED INTO LITTLE SCHOOLS?

Once the decision to form schools within a school has been made, the method of separating pupils must be determined. The methods are discussed below with illustrations of schools using each method.

Vertical organization

Students from each grade in the school are divided equally and assigned to a unit so that each unit has pupils from each grade. The pupils remain in the same little school until they graduate or leave school. Vertical assignment allows pupils to mingle with others of different maturity levels. It is less affected by varying grade enrollments than other methods of organization. For example, a large increase in the sophomore class enrollment is divided among the several units.

Vertical organization has the added advantage of having pupils and their classroom teachers remain together for more than one year, if pupils are scheduled for classes within the little school. If this is done, the number of pupils assigned to a unit can be coordinated with the number of pupils needed for the sections planned. Furthermore, teachers may instruct classes for more than one grade while remaining attached to the same little school.

The Newton High Schools, Newton, Massachusetts, are examples of schools decentralized vertically. When they were visited in November, 1960, approximately 400 pupils were enrolled in each of the six units at Newton High, while the two units at Newton South enrolled about 600 pupils each. Newton South was considering three little schools of 500 pupils for the 1961–62 school year. The units at both schools enroll pupils in grades 10–12.

21

The Andrew Warde and Roger Ludlowe High Schools in Fairfield, Connecticut, enroll pupils of grades 9–12 in their decentralized units. Four little schools are organized at each high school in buildings designed to accommodate up to 1500 pupils per site.

Horizontal organization

Using this plan a school's enrollment is separated by grade level, with each grade forming a unit. For example, ninth-graders comprise one unit, tenth-graders comprise another unit, and so forth. Horizontal assignment emphasizes pupil relationships at one grade. An increased enrollment in any grade will make the size of the little schools uneven. If a school wishes to emphasize curriculum integration at each grade level, horizontal organization is favorable.

The Brookline, Massachusetts, High School has decentralized horizontally since 1934. The pupil population of more than 2200 is divided into one unit for each grade, 9 through 12. Each little school has a name, a banner, a motto, and a color scheme. The units are named for men who made significant contributions to local history.

In Atlanta, Georgia, a high school favoring decentralization has separated its pupils horizontally, just as it did when it was a junior high school. The nine little schools, of 160 pupils each, at William A. Bass Junior High became five units of 200 pupils each as the school converted to a senior high school.

2-2 organization

By combining the vertical and horizontal methods of pupil separation, this method places two grades in each little school. While usually ninth and tenth graders are in one unit and eleventh and twelfth graders in the other, junior-senior high schools have been organized with a unit of seventh and eighth graders added to the above, producing a 2-2-2 organization.

The Pennsbury High School, Fallsington, Pennsylvania, has

used 2-2-2 organization since its formation in 1948. Presently consisting of four secondary schools on two sites, Pennsbury's unique organization enables it to focus on two years of the secondary school curriculum in each school.

Team groups

To further capitalize on smaller-group possibilities for individual attention and integration of subject matter, schools have organized teaching teams within the little-school structure. This enables a small group of teachers to concentrate on a more limited number of pupils than are enrolled in the unit.

For example, at Pennsbury the teaching team is called a grade-level group. As the name implies, pupils in a grade are divided into groups of 150 to 180 and attend classes only with students from their group. The six to eight teachers assigned to a group teach classes composed of students solely or largely from their group. Central to the groups' success are grade-level group meetings involving all teachers working with the group. The meetings, as well as the entire organization, attempt to focus upon pupil growth. To this end, staff members aim at the solution of problems involved in the improvement of teaching and learning.

Six school districts in California, including high schools and junior high schools, are using teaching team groups in a plan similar to Pennsbury's. These schools, as part of a Claremont Graduate School research project, began team groups on the premise that routines in large schools are generally well organized but seldom provide the flexibility and individual concern which builds a sense of personal responsibility among students. One goal of the teams, therefore, is to retain the flexibility and personal concern of the small high school. Early results of this comprehensive study indicate three primary requisites for success of the organization: leadership ability in the team leader, ability of the teachers to work together, and sufficient administrative and parental support (6).

23

PROGRAM—WHAT CURRICULA AND SERVICES
SHOULD EACH LITTLE SCHOOL OFFER?

Classes

Ideally, to gain the greatest advantages of personal relationships, a pupil's classes in a school within a school should all be scheduled with students and teachers in his unit. Ability grouping and a breadth of elective subjects, however, make the ideal economically difficult. Schools that do attempt to schedule a pupil's classes within the little-school unit realize, therefore, that a pupil will leave his unit for more classes as he progresses from grade 7 to grade 12. An accepted policy is to schedule each pupil for the most suitable program, disregarding the number of classes he will have within his unit.

Schedules of pupils in the horizontally organized Brookline, Massachusetts, High School are established within the unit as much as possible. The resulting schedule of classes places a student almost exclusively with others from his unit in required courses, such as English. In elective courses open to all grades, the enrollment includes members of any unit. Students from all little schools associate in the cafeteria.

In contrast, pupils in the Scarsdale, New York, Junior High School have all academic subjects plus art and vocal music within their unit. At Scarsdale, the little schools are arranged vertically through grades 6, 7, and 8. Each contains about 340 pupils.

The vertically organized Andrew Warde High School seeks to schedule an optimum number of pupils for classes within their little schools. Hodgson's study (23) showed that in one year 66 per cent of the freshmen, 50 per cent of the sophomores, 44 per cent of the juniors, and 18 per cent of the seniors had three or more classes within their unit. While this declining percentage over a four-year period is representative, nevertheless for a school with a strong commitment to ability grouping, the percentages are favorable.

In a number of schools that decentralize other phases of their organization, classes are assigned without regard for little-school identity. Such institutions choose instead to concentrate on refinement of ability grouping techniques, extension of breadth of course offerings, and development of guidance services offered to the pupils. In addition, by having schedule cards prepared by a unit staff member who knows the capabilities and personality traits of pupils and teachers, these schools improve their assignments.

Larger schools such as Newton, Evanston, White Plains, and Forest Hills, enrolling from 2500 to over 4000, are among those that minimize scheduling pupils within their units. Machine scheduling may push them further in this direction. The perfecting of teaching team groups, however, is a promising development for such schools to investigate.

High school vs. junior high scheduling

The junior high school program, by its number of required courses, lends itself more to assigning pupils to classes within their little schools than does the high school program. With less emphasis on specialized education and ability grouping in the junior high years, assignment to most courses within one's unit can become a reality.

Assignment to classes at Scarsdale Junior High School has already been noted. Similarly, at Woodrow Wilson Junior High School, pupils attend class within their little school except for music, physical education, and industrial arts. A like plan is in effect at the Lower Merion School District in Ardmore, Pennsylvania.

25

Administration and guidance

While there is little uniformity about scheduling pupils to classes within their units, there is concentration of administration and guidance services. Administration lies within the little schools without exception; guidance becomes a unit responsibility in most schools within a school.

The little school's key role in administration and guidance of pupils in a decentralized high school is indicated by this statement detailing the unit (division) functions at White Plains High School:

1. Inducting and orienting pupils to the division, the school and the community,
2. Developing and maintaining esprit de corps within the division with loyalties to the division, the school and the community,
3. Providing the counseling and guidance necessary to enable each pupil to participate in and to attain optimal profit from those school experiences which will result in the maximum development of his native and acquired abilities, talents (be they mental or manual), knowledges and skills,
4. Providing the data and counseling necessary for each pupil to understand his peculiar interests, abilities and talents and for him to plan and succeed in activities that will lead to a rich and fruitful life, both as an individual and a contributing citizen in a free society,
5. Providing a program of student activities which will be of interest and value to each pupil including, among others, student participation in divisional and school government, special interest clubs, appropriate social activities, intra-mural athletics, and certain appropriate inter-scholastic athletics,
6. Providing a program of parent education and home contacts which will give adequate understanding of and support for the educational activities of the division and the school,
7. Coordinating divisional policies, programs, activities and procedures with the policies, programs, activities and procedures of the entire school,
8. Administering operational personnel records for pupils and teachers assigned to the division,
9. Administering attendance records and carrying out such activities as are necessary to ensure that each pupil meets state and local requirements,

26

10. Administering necessary and appropriate disciplinary actions, and
11. Supervising maintenance and safety activities in those sections of the building and campus assigned for divisional use (18).

If a school within a school is to complete such functions, adequate personnel and satisfactory leadership are requisites. Job responsibilities of little-school staff members will be specified in Chapter 4. It should be noted here, however, that a leader is responsible for each unit. This leader has the services of one or more full-time or part-time counselors to perform the guidance functions. The trend seems to be toward full-time counselors rather than teacher-counselors.

When the little school performs guidance functions, a pupil remains with the same counselor throughout his years in school. Pupil records and guidance notes are kept within the unit office rather than in a central school office. The unit office becomes the heart of school activities for the boys and girls assigned to that little school.

For example, each pupil enrolled at Evanston Township High School is assigned to a unit and to a homeroom within the unit. The pupil remains in this unit during his years at Evanston. His locker, study hall, and attendance office are located in the building quadrant designated for his school within the school. Each pupil is also assigned to a counselor, who is available to his students during the daily homeroom period as well as at other times when the student is not in class. This counseling relationship continues over a four-year period. In matters relating to attendance, discipline, and general school problems, the pupil consults with his unit principal or the secretary in the unit office.

If, as at Brookline, counselors are not assigned within a little school, they draw pupils from more than one of the units. Since the full-time counselors at Brookline have pupils from each grade, they associate with four units. Because the unit principal (housemaster) has final responsibility for the program of subjects carried by each student in his unit, he and the counselors confer frequently about students. Supervision of counselors, nevertheless, lies with a head counselor rather than with the unit principal.

ENROLLMENT—WHAT SIZE SHOULD THE LITTLE SCHOOL BE?

A necessarily early decision that a principal and staff forming little schools must make concerns enrollment limits. This judgment affects the pupil organization, the educational program, and the guidance organization to be used. Many schools have units in the 400- to 600-pupil range. Others are known to operate with as few as 125 or as many as 1100 pupils in a unit.

In general, the little schools seem proportionate in size to the total enrollment. If the total school enrolls under 1000 pupils, its little schools enroll less than 350. If the total school enrolls 1000 to 2500 pupils, its units enroll 350 to 700. If the total school enrolls over 2500 pupils, its units enroll more than 700.

Just as a principal and staff decide that their total school is too large and therefore they will decentralize, so also must they determine enrollment limits for the smaller units. Forming answers to the questions that have been asked in this chapter will help them. A review in Chapter 4 of how job responsibilities may be assigned in little schools should also furnish assistance.

Job Descriptions
for Schools Within Schools

THIS CHAPTER DESCRIBES INDIVIDUAL RELATIONSHIPS WITHIN THE organizational structure of little schools. In studying these personnel assignments, it bears reemphasis that the structure's fundamental purpose is to bring an improved quality of staff attention to each pupil. Close teacher cooperation, desirable in all schools, becomes essential. Subject-matter individualism of teachers must be lessened through continuous personnel screening and in-service training.

ORGANIZATION CHARTS

To aid in clarifying job relationships, organization charts are shown on pages 30–33. The charts illustrate current practice in institutions using the little-school plan. They show that job titles are not standardized in these schools; this hampers a comparison of responsibilities. In order to proceed, however, titles are assigned and the positions are described below. This action supports the belief of Griffiths and others that the job description offers the advantage of greater teamwork, security to all staff personnel, and greater utilization of staff members' abilities (21).

Figure 1 shows the administrative organization chart at Azusa High School, Azusa, California (over 2000 pupils). Figure 2 shows

Figure 1. AZUSA HIGH SCHOOL—ADMINISTRATIVE ORGANIZATION

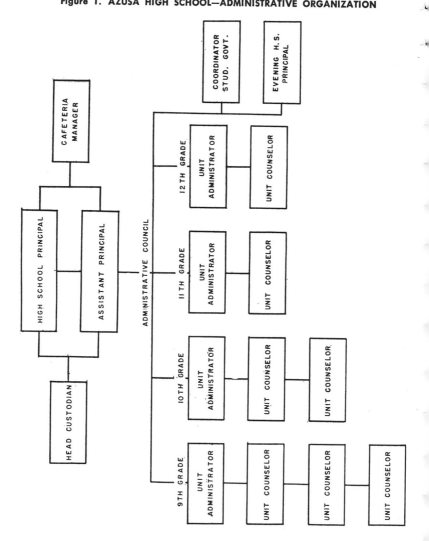

Figure 2. SCARSDALE JUNIOR HIGH SCHOOL—ADMINISTRATIVE ORGANIZATION

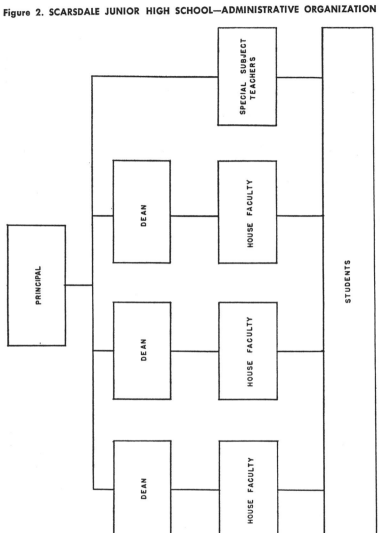

Figure 3. EVANSTON TOWNSHIP HIGH SCHOOL—ADMINISTRATIVE ORGANIZATION

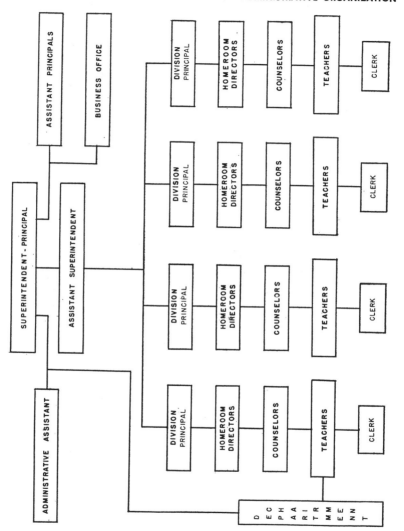

Figure 4. TOPEKA WEST HIGH SCHOOL—ADMINISTRATIVE ORGANIZATION

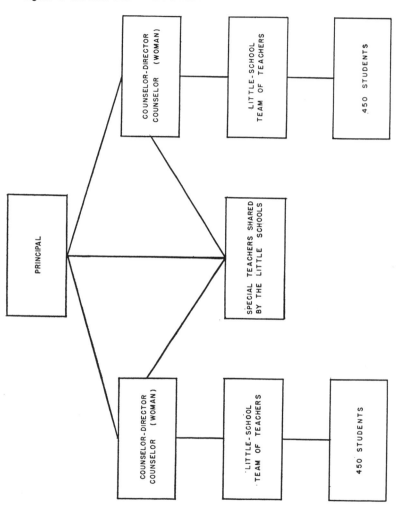

the organization of the Scarsdale, New York, Junior High School (over 1000). Figure 3 indicates how the Evanston, Illinois, Township High School (over 4000 pupils) is organized. Figure 4 represents the organization at the new Topeka, Kansas, West High School, which accommodates about 1500 pupils.

PRINCIPAL (Headmaster) *

The principal retains ultimate accountability for operating the school and is assigned general responsibility for instructional supervision, curriculum development, plant management, student control, community relations, and guidance of students. Hopefully, by delegating functions to little-school personnel, he gains the time needed to lead the staff in these areas. Austin, French, and Hull offer these suggestions to help the principal get to the heart of his job:

. . . improving instruction, broadly but not vaguely defined, should constantly be the chief goal of the principal, and he should budget his time thoughtfully and spend it intelligently to that end. He should make a schedule for himself and learn to maintain it by delegating less important matters to others and by dispatching promptly all business that he undertakes (5:148).

Similarly, a Philadelphia Suburban School Study Council committee recommended that principals at member schools, to have time for instructional improvement, should replace the open-door policy with a planned and structured work day. This would allow principals to set aside definite hours for visits to classrooms (27).

Student control and guidance of pupils are usually delegated to the little-school staffs. Other principalship duties may be assigned to unit leaders or to an assistant principal, acting within a mutually established policy framework.

* Similar position titles are shown in parentheses.

By design, however, the principal retains direct leadership of curriculum development and instructional supervision. He must see that vertical curriculum coordination occurs in each subject; he accomplishes this through department chairmen. In an organization without department chairmen, the principal may appoint rotating department chairmen, may delegate this responsibility to little-school administrators, or may develop coordination through system-wide supervisors.

As the high school increases in enrollment, its principal is likely to gain administrative help in addition to the little-school administrators. School districts do not act uniformly in this matter, however. For example, three schools are organized as little schools, each dividing into four units. In addition to an administrator in charge of each unit, the 1500-pupil school has one full-time assistant principal; the 2200-pupil school has two full-time assistant principals; the 2250-pupil school has no assistant principals.

ASSISTANT PRINCIPAL (Assistant headmaster, administrative assistant)

As illustrated by the charts, the assistant principal may serve in either a line or a staff role. He may be delegated direct supervision of unit principals, in addition to performing other general administrative duties. Such is the case at the 1500-pupil Newark, Ohio, High School, where the assistant principal supervises the three building coordinators. Matters involving more than one of the little schools, such as scheduling and extracurricular activities, are his direct responsibility (24).

The assistant principal performs more customary duties of a staff nature in other decentralized high schools. In the Fairfield, Connecticut, high schools, however, the assistant headmaster (principal) assumes direct responsibility for guidance as indicated by these assigned tasks:

35

1. Development of the school guidance program including such activities as in-service education, coordination with system-wide guidance program, follow-up studies of graduates and non-graduates, reporting and analysis of standardized testing and College Entrance examinations.
2. Resource person to the house staff in the development and improvement of house guidance program.
3. Counselor for those pupils requiring unusual specialized guidance (for example, college admission, psychological counseling, and vocational placement).
4. Coordinator of the school guidance program and directly related activities (23:69).

Directly or indirectly, the assistant principal may contribute to increased supervision in the instructional program, either by participating personally or by relieving the principal so that he may supervise. If the assistant serves as a general assistant to the principal in all of the principal's coordinating activities, he, like the principal, can become a unifying factor throughout the school.

UNIT PRINCIPAL * (Division principal, housemaster, division director, building coordinator, dean)

The unit principals are directly responsible to the principal or his assistant, who prescribes their work through regularly scheduled meetings within an established framework of school policy. The unit principals exercise judgment within the framework; they are encouraged to be creative in completing their duties.

Since this position, designed as a limited principalship, is unique to schools within a school, the division (unit) principal's job description as set forth at Evanston Township High School is quoted below. The duties are related to three groups. Regarding students:

The division principal would be informed concerning all possible sources of help regarding any problem within the province of the

* Title preferred by writer. If little schools were called houses, the title would be house principal.

school. He could make proper referral to the person best able to be of help. In his many contacts with parents he would have a personal acquaintanceship with them. In cases of discipline, he would probably handle the problem, recognizing that most discipline problems require counseling (15:18).

With respect to teacher associates of the division, the division principal was to take the lead:

1. In providing identification with the division of the staff group and of the students and parents of the division
2. In organizing in-service development activities involving:
   a. Evaluation of educational program
   b. Appraisal of school organization
   c. Study and understanding of students and student needs
   d. Modification of curriculum and activity program
3. In providing through meetings of the division staff associates the opportunity for:
   a. Learning of plans and developments in the various school departments, all of which should be represented on the staff of each division
   b. Securing information about and interpretation of school-wide objectives and policies
   c. Deliberating on matters posed for school staff reaction and decision, including those which may be posed to the group by individual staff members of the division (15:10).

With respect to his relationship with the central administration, the division principal was to:

1. Serve with the superintendent-principal, the assistant principal, the other division principals, the business manager, and the coordinator of curriculum and counseling as the staff executive committee for Evanston Township High School *
2. See that school plans and programs considered by central administration and the Board of Education would take into account the characteristics and feelings of pupils and parents as studied and understood through cooperation of the division
3. Assume responsibility, additional to that for administration of the division, for some special area of central staff administrative service such as student teaching program, adult education, summer school program, staff personnel, student personnel services, school public relations, program, etc. (15:10).

* As shown in Figure 3, the positions of assistant superintendent and administrative assistant and another assistant principal have been added.

37

As specified above and as evolved at other schools using the little-school plan, the unit principal's functions are comprehensive. He must know the pupils and the opportunities the school offers if the system is to succeed.

Student control becomes a prime task. If the administrator knows the pupils and their backgrounds, preventive discipline is more possible than in schools where the disciplinarians are farther removed from the students. To supplement his knowledge of pupils and staff, the unit principal will visit classes.

At Newton High School, Newton, Massachusetts, each unit has a student problems committee to assist the unit principal in decisions regarding involved and persistent behavior problems. Committee members include counselors, the unit principal, and representatives selected by the unit principal from the unit faculty. In addition to consulting with the unit principal, this group makes recommendations when long-term suspensions and expulsion are being considered.

In working with pupils in daily operating situations, at most schools, the unit principal's function is dually administration and guidance. He tests the axiom that "to effectively counsel, one cannot set penalties for pupil misbehavior." Although his responsibility in guidance may be limited to supervision of counselors reporting to him, when he meets with pupils and parents the educational program and future plans are often discussed.

At Brookline, the unit principal's guidance function becomes direct in that he assigns pupils in his unit to classes after the master schedule has been prepared. This assignment was first begun in 1941, and the number of pupil failures during the 1941–42 school year was reduced by 20 per cent from 1940–41. Since the unit principal's ability in assigning pupils was considered directly related to lowering the failures, this duty has been continued.

Because the unit principal participates personally in both administration and guidance of students, enrollment in the little

38

school affects the degree of success he is likely to have and the number of other functions he will be free to perform. As the number of pupils increases, he will have less time for other duties if he is to maintain the same degree of knowledge of individual pupils.

The previously quoted Evanston job description and the organizational charts indicate that unit principals have a supervisory role in relation to both teachers and counselors. In working with teachers, where departmental organization exists, the unit principal will most often supervise teachers in matters of student control while the department chairman will supervise instruction and subject matter coordination. If no department organization exists, the unit principal may assume the supervision of instruction jointly with the school principal. Although most schools have placed guidance personnel within the unit's supervisory and operational context, where this is not the case a guidance chairman assumes supervision of counselors.

To add to other duties, a unit principal may also teach one or more classes. Generally, however, teaching is not included in the job responsibilities.

While in most schools the unit principal remains in his position indefinitely, Brookline uses a different plan. A unit principal is appointed on a year-to-year basis, but he may not serve more than four years. This policy was instituted for three reasons: (a) when a person knows that he can serve only a specific term, he will give that term all of his skill and ability; (b) if the position were permanently assigned, this door to administration would be closed to all others, some of whom might prove to be better; (c) the housemaster who returns to full-time teaching promotes better teacher-administrator relationships because of his knowledge of administrative problems (7).

Those who believe that satisfactory service merits a second term question the above policy. Experienced unit principals are particularly needed if there is no other full-time administrator in the building. In the 1960–61 school year all unit principals at Brookline had served a previous time, but no one had ever received two consecutive sets of appointments.

With qualified people serving as unit principals, the units can bring flexibility and innovation to the school's administration. Although a new idea might not be tried with 2000 pupils, the same idea would more likely be used if only one-fourth that number were involved.

UNIT ASSISTANT (Division assistant)

Where this position exists in a school's organizational structure, the person's duties and abilities are designed to complement the unit principal's. The assistant will have teaching responsibilities in addition to unit tasks. At several schools, duties in the unit student activity program fall to the assistant.

COUNSELORS

Typically belonging to the little-school organization, counselors report directly to the unit principal. In the few schools where they are not serving a specific unit, counselors are supervised by the guidance chairman.

Counselors may be assigned vertically, having students from all grades in the unit, or their counselees may all come from one grade. There is no trend in this matter. No matter what the assignment method, though, the pupil remains with the counselor throughout his high school career.

Schools within a school seem to favor full-time rather than part-time counselors. Yet the new White Plains Senior High School has established a singular organization and facilities for teacher-counselors, which is described in detail in the next paragraphs.

Because of the principal's belief that an increasing air of

mystery about guidance should be removed, the teacher-counselors daily meet with students in homeroom and individual situations. They are immediately concerned with discovering the general and personal needs of students and deciding the best ways of meeting them (41). Teacher-counselors are allowed four periods of an eight-period day for counseling.

As originally established, there were ten teacher-counselor groups in each little school of 550 pupils. These groups, including students from each grade, have daily noon meetings. Since no classes are held from twelve to one o'clock, all students divide the time between their teacher-counselor groups and the cafeterias. They switch locations after thirty minutes.

Guidance in program making, activities, adjustments, and plans for each student at White Plains begins with his teacher-counselor. Of immediate secondary assistance are the unit principal, the college counselor, the psychologist, and the coordinator of pupil personnel services.

The provision of facilities for guidance personnel in each little school at White Plains deserves special mention. Each unit contains a series of ten teacher-counselor offices adjacent to the multipurpose room. The offices are unique in that each has a telephone. Thus it is theoretically possible for the school's entire staff of forty teacher-counselors simultaneously to have private face-to-face or telephone conferences.

While other schools use a noon-hour homeroom arrangement similar to that at White Plains, the more common plan is to have a ten-minute homeroom session earlier in the day. As with counselors, homeroom teachers are usually assigned to a specific unit and serve a group of pupils as long as that group is in school.

Several decentralized schools, especially junior high schools, emphasize the teacher's role in guidance more than that of a full-time or part-time specialist. Through teacher team groups having the same period free for planning together, parent and student conferences can be held at one time with all teachers

41

who daily work with an individual pupil. This plan is used at the Ardmore Junior High School in Ardmore, Pennsylvania.

Similarly, the weekly case conference period at Brookline High School shows how unit staff members work with other school personnel to aid individual students. Every Wednesday morning for three hours, the principal, the school doctors, the head counselor, the adjustment counselor, and the unit principal and counselor of students to be discussed have a series of case conferences. Although often the case involves a persistent discipline problem, other types of chronic problems, such as underachievers, may be brought before the group.

We have indicated that schools using the little-school plan favor full-time counselors specifically attached to one unit. The counselor will deal directly with a group of 250 to 300 pupils. Pupil records are located in the unit office. The satisfaction of one principal whose school is organized in this way is evident in this concluding paragraph from his letter to the writer:

> The morale of the student body is high; the respect for the school and school property is evident. The hopes for a great future are expressed continually. The assistant principal and I are able to spend a good bit of time not only in supervision of instruction, but in meeting with both faculty and pupils for individual, group, and multiple counseling. In my opinion, the A. C. Flora High School is perfectly designed for guidance which makes it also well designed for efficient teaching and good learning.*

DEPARTMENT CHAIRMEN

The organization charts show that schools within a school may abandon departmental organization. Where chairmen exist, they are responsible to the principal or his assistant for completing duties similar to those of department heads elsewhere. Ordinarily in such schools the chairmen, principal, and unit principals will

---

* Letter to the writer from J. K. Blum, principal, A. C. Flora High School, Columbia, South Carolina, January 10, 1961.

form a curriculum council to coordinate policy. In such groups, because of their close association with pupils, the unit principals can comment on the effect curriculum proposals would have on their students.

If there are no department chairmen, curriculum integration and routine department chores fall elsewhere in the administrative team. One possible arrangement is that used at the Ardmore Junior High School, where the department chairmanship is rotated. No teacher assumes this duty for more than two years. The chairman's tasks include vertical curriculum development within one subject and recommendation of instructional materials and books.

TEACHERS

Teachers in a decentralized school have allegiance both to their subject field and to the total school, as do teachers elsewhere. In schools within a school, however, the teachers' overall responsibility becomes more limited. At Evanston Township High School the teachers' position is described this way:

. . . insofar as possible two basic attachments should be provided in the assignment of each staff member: one in terms of the area of his special field and one oriented, through the division and the school as a whole, to common membership concerned with cooperatively understanding and serving the total educational needs of the secondary-school youth of the community (15:9).

The teacher's fundamental task of instruction may be completed within the classroom of a single unit. To do so is the aim at many schools, but the limitations of ability grouping and elective courses have already been noted. In addition to teaching, duties such as activity supervision, building supervision, homeroom direction, and faculty meeting attendance may be organized by units. Assigning the latter activities by unit is of underlying importance, where teaching is not done within the unit, if teacher-unit identification is to grow. Continuing teacher-

43

unit assignments beyond one year is desirable for the same reason.

The total school faculty may be divided among the little schools in several ways. The group may be separated equally by departments, regardless of teaching assignment. Or, an equal division can be established according to location in the building. Where teaching is done within the unit structure, the required-subject teachers may be divided equally and the elective-subject teachers may form another group.

At Bellflower, California, the last plan seems best suited to school needs. Bellflower High's principal tells of its plan and its special advantages to him in stating:

. . . in our particular set-up—and we hold no brief for this—there is a group of teachers who deal strictly with elective subjects and are not assigned to a sub-school. This group is assigned to me. So, in effect, we have three student groups but we have four teacher groups. We have four administrators—the three sub-school principals and myself—each of whom has a group of teachers with whom to work. This relieves me of the necessity of visiting a lot of teachers and allows me to concentrate on the smaller number handling the electives. I visit these classes and I think I'm doing a better job because I'm not trying to cover such a large area (39:36).

Just as faculty members are assigned to units by several methods, so also are there varying opinions about the optimal number of members for a unit faculty. It is evident, however, that as the pupil enrollment of a unit must be limited if the unit principal is to know all of the students, so also the number of faculty must be limited according to the duties assigned the unit principal.

SECRETARY

Secretarial and clerical assistance extends the promise of the unit plan, as it will other patterns of organization. Since attendance procedures flow through the unit office, clerical details of attendance are a daily task for the secretary. One helpful attendance practice is to have the secretary telephone the homes of absent pupils each day.

Maturity in the little-school secretary is essential. She contacts many pupils daily about attendance and other matters which are a part of unit administrative details. A firm word from the secretary can conserve the unit principal's time. If a secretary remains in this position for several years, she can become an effective member of the unit team and a valued friend of many pupils.

AIDE

This position was first developed at Newton High School. The aide is a noncertified, nonsecretarical employee whose primary duties are to relieve the unit principal of routine tasks and to assist unit teachers. Employed half-time, the aide may execute minor administrative procedures, supervise study halls, or do other jobs that the unit principal feels will improve the organization. The aide's services are designed to free the unit principal and teachers for significant personal relationships with students and faculty.

SUMMARY AND COMPARISON

The discussion of organizational structure in Chapter 3 and the job descriptions in the present chapter affirm the number of a little-school staff who have continuing relationships with pupils. Continuity of staff and maintaining pupils in designated areas of the building help to develop a sense of belonging in the pupils. To summarize Chapters 3 and 4, and to relate little-school organization to accepted principles of organization, the principles stated in Chapter 2 are repeated and commented upon.

Principle 1: Organization Structure
An organizational structure is necessary when any group has a common task.

The institutions established as little schools appear to have fundamentally accepted this principle. Although parts of their organization are not time-tested, the underlying structure seems firmly established. Decentralization is the key to organization at each institution.

The organizational structure where little schools are used, following the pattern in education throughout the country, adheres to line and staff design. Little-school administrators are uniformly line officials.

Principle 2: Unity of Purpose
The purposes and objectives of an organization must be determined and understood.

On examination of literature about organization and personnel in schools that use the little-school plan, an evident force in each institution is interest in the individual pupil's welfare. This interest, vital to the development of every youngster at which the schools aim, may cause the formation of smaller units at different stages in enrollment growth. Yet the stated purpose whenever decentralization occurs is the same: greater benefit to the individual.

Principle 3: Division of Work
The scheme of organization should provide for maximum homogeneity in the division of work.

Since schools within a school are new in many communities, the work load assigned to positions in the organization is receiving continuing study. For example, how should the enrollment in a little-school unit affect the responsibilities of its administrator? To what degree shall guidance become a specialized function of counselors? A faculty's answer to these questions establishes the degree of uniformity in the work of teachers, counselors, and administrators.

46

Principle 4: Coordination
Coordination of functions, activities, interest, and assignments is necessary for successful accomplishment of results.

Primary responsibility for coordination in this plan of organization remains with the principal. Directly responsible to him or his assistant are administrators heading the units. Although their duties vary with the school, each unit principal has tasks relating to attendance and student control.

Pertinent to student control are the enrollment in each school within the school, other duties assigned to its principal, and staff assistance given him. Enrollments in units are known to range from 125 to 1100. Coordination of curriculum matters, directly supervised by the principal of the school, typically is channeled to the teachers through department heads. A similar plan functions in guidance.

Meetings are the chief device used by the head administrator at each institution to coordinate unit principals, department chairmen, and guidance chairmen. Unit principals normally attend all meetings, while the others commonly are present only when their specialty is under consideration.

Principle 5: Single Executive
Every organization should have a single executive head.

To the writer's knowledge, decentralized schools adhere to this uniformly.

Principle 6: Span of Control
One executive can only deal effectively with a limited number of persons.

The chief high school executive's span of control varies. He typically deals directly with his assistants and with little-school principals. Department heads, guidance chairmen, administrative assistants, and staff specialists, however, may report to the principal.

47

Principle 7: Authority and Responsibility
The necessary authority to accomplish a task should be delegated at the same time the responsibility for the task is assigned; every person in the organization should know to whom and for what he is responsible, and no individual in the organization should be required to take direct orders from more than one person.

One must work in an institution in order to speak with authority about the first part of this principle. There is nothing in the organizational structure, nevertheless, to prevent proper delegation of authority.

Of great assistance in adhering to the second part, knowing to whom and for what one is responsible, are the job descriptions developed by schools in originating or revising their little-school plans. As noted earlier, Griffiths and others definitely favor pre-employment job descriptions. They support their position by saying:

. . . if modern leadership theory is at all correct, . . . an administrator is not "good" in isolation, but in reference to a situation. Thus, if we are to have effective administrators, we must first describe the situation and then find the man who can fill its requirements (21:150).

The degree to which personnel in schools within a school must take direct orders from more than one person relates to the amount of centralization and job specialization. Where department heads exist, teachers are responsible to them for classroom performance and to little-school principals for homeroom duties, teacher-counselor tasks, and services as an activity sponsor. Counselors are in a similar position where made responsible to a guidance head. Most progress in eliminating dual responsibility seems to have occurred in schools where department-head authority is vested in the little-school principals.

Principle 8: Planning and Decision-Making
Every organization must make provision for effective planning and decision-making.

The primary sources of planning and decision-making at
48

each school are meetings of the principal with little-school principals, department heads, and guidance chairmen. Also, there are meetings of departments and groups within each unit. To improve the school's focus on individual pupils, meetings of team groups are a promising way for faculties to communicate about pupils.

Principle 9: Flexibility
   Policies and terms should be stated in terms broad enough to permit reasonable flexibility in management.
Principle 10: Stability
   Continuity of policy and program until results can be evaluated is a prerequisite to good management.

Investigation shows that schools having the little-school plan attempt to encourage flexibility and innovation within the units. For example, although policies affecting attendance and student control are necessarily identical within the units, administrators exercise judgment within the policy framework. Similarly, the institutions seem to be striving for continuity while encouraging inventiveness.

Principle 11: Production
   An effective organization must attain its goal if it is to survive.
Principle 12: Evaluation
   Evaluation is essential to the progress of any group. (28:54–61)

While several schools have written of their organization's values, to the writer's knowledge little schools have lacked a comprehensive evaluation. At least two communities have suggested that evaluation should take place only after a graduating class has completed its entire high school career under the new system.

Creative, dedicated staff members are fundamental to the little-school plan, as they are to any form of organization. To realize staff potential fully, job descriptions are written indicating responsibilities and relationships in the organization. The past two chapters have told how staffs are organized and relate in

49

schools within a school. Functioning on sound principles, knowing how to associate within the structure, little-school staffs have the background to focus on individual pupils. The next chapter describes facilities used to aid them in their efforts.

Facilities for
Schools Within Schools

PROPER FACILITIES ARE HELPFUL TO THE SCHOOLS-WITHIN-A-SCHOOL plan. Since the individual student is the focal point of interest and concern, the school plant should indicate this student emphasis. Chapter 5 will trace the development of facilities augmenting little-school organization and indicate fundamental building needs.

STUDY HALL TO GENERAL EDUCATION LABORATORY

A large space for common use was the first facility characteristic of institutions using little schools. Beginning with the 250-pupil capacity homeroom-study halls at Evanston, the large spaces gained versatility when a general education laboratory was installed at Beacon, New York. Here the area could be used for planning and research, large-group audiovisual presentations, and dramatic productions. Designs for decentralized schools in the early 1950's also often included a large general room.

Hodgson's study reported further use of large spaces in describing Syosset High School in 1958:

In the center of each unit was a large area about three classrooms in size which was known at Syosset as the project area. It served as a student commons, area for large class instruction, study hall, and as an area for small class groups or individuals to work on various activities. . . .

Adjacent to the unit library at one end of the project area was a teacher's workroom, the dean's office and a small office. . . . The project area was equipped with round, square and trapezoidal tables and chairs. Available in each unit and from a central storage area were additional folding chairs. . . . Art supplies, tape recorders, projectors, phonographs, etc., were available in each of the little schools for use in the classroom or the project area (23:158).

Later pages in this chapter will discuss and illustrate the newest proposals for using large spaces in schools within a school. The reader should note in examples that follow, however, that decentralized schools do use large spaces in each unit to relate the pupil to his unit. The spaces also contribute to individualizing the educational program, if flexibility is encouraged in teaching methods and teacher utilization.

OLDER BUILDINGS HAVING SCHOOLS WITHIN A SCHOOL

Chapter 2 reviewed institutions that pioneered little school organization; in them, the organizational plan had to fit in existing buildings. Currently many communities have older buildings that they continue to use; this section describes and diagrams unit facilities in two such buildings. In these and in others, classrooms have been successfully converted into offices or common rooms, aiding the organizational plan.

Evanston Township High School

The school plant was built in stages according to a master plan suggested more than thirty years ago (34). Figure 5 shows the floor plan in September, 1961, indicating the stages of development. As noted in Chapter 2, the little-school plan began with the use of the large homeroom-study halls. Each three-story wing contained three of these spaces. Homeroom locations are shown by the numbers 104, 124, 144, and 164 on the diagram, with corresponding rooms on the other floors.

Figure 5. EVANSTON TOWNSHIP HIGH SCHOOL—SCHOOL PLAN

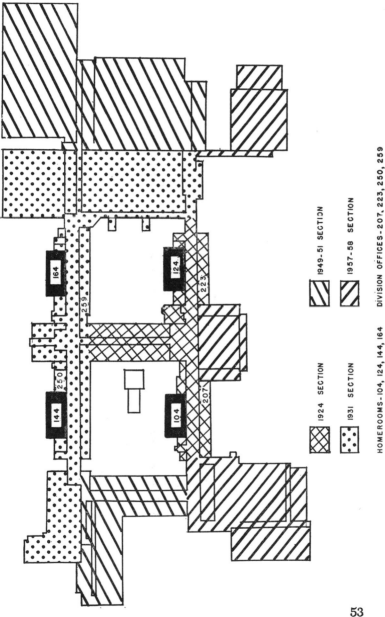

Central to this discussion is a description of physical facilities used solely by the divisions.* Each division has as "home base" one quadrant of the building, including the homerooms and the office in that quadrant. Eight homeroom-study halls were used in 1961–62, the third-floor rooms having been refurbished for large-group instruction and team-teaching projects.

The homerooms contained 250 stationary pupil desks. These are arranged in twenty-six rows across the room's breadth, with nine or ten desks per row. Each room has its own distinctive features. At one end is a private office usually assigned to the division assistant, who uses the office singly or shares it.

Each little-school office is located on the second floor. These areas, reconverted classrooms, are divided into three parts: (a) a small private office at one end for the division principal; (b) a larger middle area for the secretary's desk, file cabinets, and the office counters; and (c) another small office at the other end for a counselor. The offices are designated 207, 223, 250, and 259 on the floor plan.

Newton High School

Newton's campus and buildings are diagrammed in Figure 6. Since the little-school offices lack a uniform pattern of location and area within the three-story buildings, the building interiors are not drawn. The areas within and adjacent to the unit office in building III, however, are drawn as representative of the six little schools. The study hall next to the office will seat seventy-five pupils scheduled from within that unit.

The commons room, furnished with comfortable furniture, is a place where students gather before and after school for meetings, for casual conversation, to play records, or to study. Each unit has a commons room with distinctive decorations and colors identifying that little school.

* The little schools at Evanston are now known as East Hall, West Hall, North Hall, and South Hall.

Figure 6. NEWTON HIGH SCHOOL—CAMPUS PLAN AND HOUSE SUITE

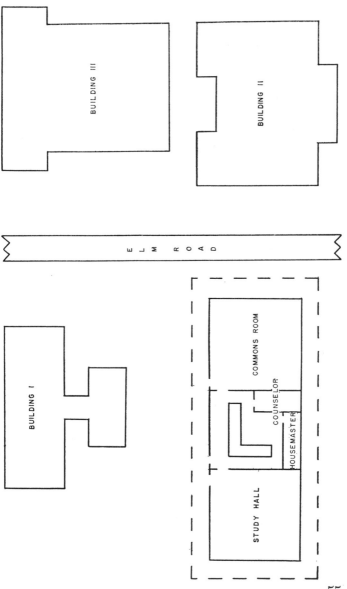

55

BUILDINGS PLANNED FOR SCHOOLS WITHIN A SCHOOL

Buildings planned to fit the philosophy of schools within a school have been designed and constructed during the last decade. Five such schools are discussed below, including one under construction and another that is a building design project. These examples show the little school emerging as a distinct building unit, designed to become the center of a pupil's academic and social life at school.

White Plains Senior High School

As the campus diagram in Figure 7 shows, this new school consists of five building segments clustered irregularly about a central unit C. The buildings are connected by enclosed arcades. The central unit contains facilities for the fine arts, sciences, industrial arts, home economics, business education, and vocational education, as well as central administrative offices and the central library.

The decentralized school plant at White Plains has two buildings, A and B, which house the facilities unique to each division. These buildings are partially described below.

1. These two buildings house academic classrooms. Each has two floors and partial basements with kitchens and storage rooms. Each of the two floors has ten classrooms and a multi-purpose room which will serve as a study hall, assembly room, group activity center and lunch room. Adjacent to this room is a food service area. About 500 sophomores, juniors, and seniors heterogeneously grouped, comprising one of the four divisions of the high school, are housed on each floor. Each division has its own conference, guidance and special work rooms.
2. Each building has been designed around a central court which will be fully landscaped to serve as an outdoor teaching, study and lunch area.
3. Food from the preparation kitchens, supplies, and equipment are brought up to the two upper levels by use of elevators.
4. The multi-purpose room is provided with a variety of types of

56

Figure 7. WHITE PLAINS SENIOR HIGH SCHOOL—CAMPUS PLAN

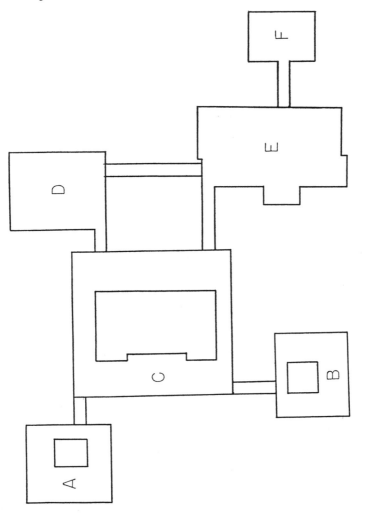

tables and seating to increase flexibility of use. The movable tables and chairs may be easily moved to the basement storage rooms by use of the elevators and the folding tables housed in the walls permitting the entire floor to be cleared if desired (11:1).

The unique teacher-counselor offices, described in Chapter 3, are located in the division buildings next to the director's office. Each pupil's locker is also placed in his little-school building.

Newton South High School

The arrangement of buildings at Newton South, as illustrated in Figure 8, consists of six two-story buildings grouped around a circular, one and one-half story library. According to Clinchy, the houses * have these characteristics:

The three houses are all two-story buildings of similar design and are equipped, for the most part, with similar facilities. However, each house will have its unique color scheme and its distinctive touches in interior arrangement and decor.

The first floor contains three language classrooms and two English classrooms of conventional size, office space for the housemaster and guidance staff, toilet facilities, and the large common room. One house has a language laboratory equipped with electronic recording and playback equipment. This will be used by the whole school.

It is the common room and the large group room which make these houses distinctive. These two spaces complement each other, the large group room providing the efficient Newton Plan benefits, the common room providing the more relaxed atmosphere which the house plan is designed to promote.

The common room, in the absence of specialized space for small group instruction, will serve for seminar groups as well as for study halls, committee meetings, relaxation, and other informal activities. It contains the branch library facilities, books and periodicals, and comfortable furniture. It will be the center of the social and personal life of the students in the house. Offices for house guidance counselors and housemasters will be just off the common room to make these people really available to the student.

* Term used at Newton rather than little school, or unit.

❋   ❋   ❋   ❋   ❋   ❋   ❋   ❋

Figure 8. NEWTON SOUTH HIGH SCHOOL—CAMPUS PLAN

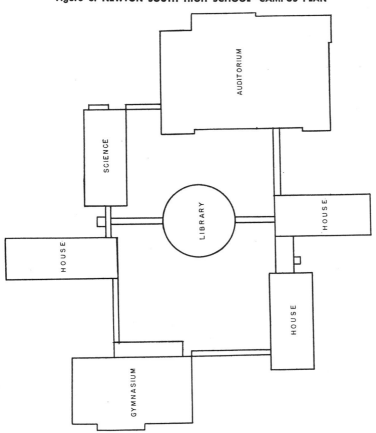

Figure 9. PLAINVIEW JUNIOR HIGH SCHOOL—UNIT PLAN

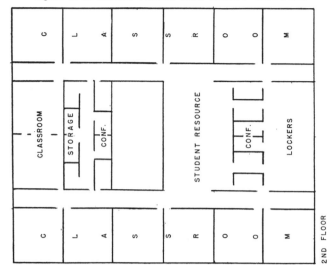

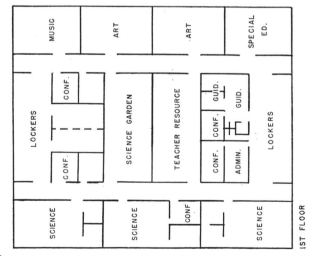

60

The second floor of this house contains three conventional math and four conventional social studies classrooms, a workroom for project work and visual teaching materials, and the large group instruction room seating up to 100 students (9:10–11).

Students from all houses jointly share the remaining buildings, including the library, the gymnasium, the science building, and the auditorium building, which contains the cafeteria. Pupils are assigned to classes, homerooms, and lockers within their houses whenever possible.

Plainview Junior High School

This 1800-pupil school has a campus layout similar to Newton South, since three little schools radiate out from a central facility. It differs from the former in having science, art, and music facilities in the units, as seen on the floor plan in Figure 9. As discussed earlier, the junior high program can be more self-contained, because of its required nature, than the senior high program. Students at Plainview, therefore, are expected to be assigned to their own units 60 to 80 per cent of the time.

Lamphere Senior High School

The faculty at this decentralized school hopes to improve its program's effectiveness for each pupil by teacher-team groups that integrate subject areas. Little schools at Lamphere are organized horizontally, with each unit having flexible space which can be used for individual, seminar, medium, or large-group instruction. A unit's floor plan and divisibility of spaces are depicted in Figure 10. It illustrates the idea of operability, which Clinchy described in a recent Educational Facilities Laboratories report. To summarize here, if a building has operability (partitions that can be moved at once and at will), it will be more economical of space and have more potential for use in operating a program for individual students (8).

61

Figure 10. LAMPHERE SENIOR HIGH SCHOOL—UNIT PLAN

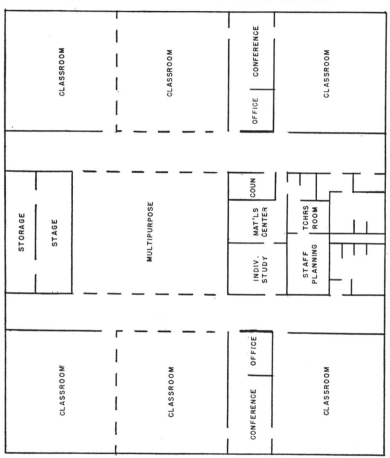

The New High School

A 16-page building design project under this title was published in *Overview* in March 1962. The project proposed to show, through architectural sketches, the little-school facilities for an institution that seriously considered the impact of Conant, Trump, and the newest technologies on its educational program. Here, then, was detailed a 900-student high school with three units. Each unit, as sketched, would have programed-learning bases, teacher offices, conference area, a reference center, and offices for the unit coordinator and his staff (31). Any reader planning facilities for schools within a school should study this article.

SUMMARY

Paralleling increasing interest in schools within a school has been the development of school plants specifically designed to enhance the plan. Older schools continue to designate a section of their building for each unit. Newer institutions, however, tend to construct the little schools in separate buildings. Both methods have proven successful when these spaces are contained in the little-school area: (a) classrooms and a workroom for unit teachers; (b) offices for the administrator and counselor; (c) a space, such as a general learning laboratory, for student groups of larger than usual class size; and (d) an area for small, private conferences.

The fundamental philosophy of schools within a school can be developed in existing buildings. Although specifically designed facilities ease development of the plan, individualized attention, personal relationships, and identification with the organization will grow where the essential spaces are provided.

CHAPTER 6

Using Schools Within Schools

THIS MONOGRAPH HAS NOW DISCUSSED THE AIM, THE DEVELOPMENT, the organization, the job descriptions, and the facilities for schools within a school. In each instance, the writer has attempted to relate theory to practice by giving examples from schools currently using little-school organization. This chapter will follow a similar format. It will appraise present use of the organization and offer guides to action for the principal and his staff.

APPRAISAL

Presumed and stated advantages

Institutions begin using the little-school plan because of advantages they presume it will bring. Others continue this organization because the advantages they find are stronger than limitations that appear. The following is a summary of the advantages as reported in three doctoral studies (Hodgson [23], Plath [35], York [43]), two informal mail surveys,* the literature,

---

* As reported in Plath, one survey was done in January, 1959, under Harold Howe II. The other survey done by Plath in December, 1960. In each, letters were sent to a selected group of educators, by states, asking for names of schools using the little-school plan. The replies received were checked by sending to the schools named for information about their organization.

correspondence, and personal interviews with individuals using the plan.

General advantage: the schools-within-a-school plan provides better attention to the individual pupil by combining the small high school's personal strengths with the larger high school's improved faculty, facilities, and curriculum.

Specific advantages:

1. To pupils:
   a. The individual pupil has closer pupil-teacher relationships. He forms friendships with the faculty personnel from his unit while retaining loyalty to the entire school; these friendships continue over a longer period of time.
   b. The guidance program improves, since individual abilities are more easily recognized and developed, cooperative staff efforts for individual pupils increase, behavior problems are recognized earlier, and the guidance program is continuous.
   c. When classes are scheduled within each unit, subject matter integration and continuity are improved.
   d. A strengthened student activities program results from increased opportunities for participation, leadership, and socialization.
   e. Removing anonymity, improving the feeling of belonging, usually results in better performance in many areas.

2. To staff:
   a. The principal is relieved of administrative routine and freed to a greater extent for true instructional leadership. At the same time, several staff members receive guided administrative experience within the little schools.
   b. A means is provided of furnishing more effective student control. The pupil feels he is known. Problem pupils and situations are recognized more easily.
   c. Teacher orientation improves, for the school can absorb a large number of new teachers more easily.

   d. Improved supervision is possible because of greater availability of the principal.

   e. School policies and faculty morale improve because of increased attention to teacher views in policy making, plus better communication.

   f. Adaptability of the educational program increases because of greater willingness to experiment within a little school.

Reactions from the field

Among those presently using the schools within a school plan, one can find a range of reactions varying from conservative praise to genuine enthusiasm. Veteran users express positive confidence, having the benefit of years of experience (40). At Brookline, where little schools have remained during the administration of three headmasters and twenty-five housemasters, a personal experience showed the writer how the little-school plan can become interwoven in the lives of both pupils and adults. When the writer was interviewing a senior student while waiting to see the principal, the student emphatically commented how happy she was that her eighth-grade brother would enter "her" house. "We have worked so hard to keep its reputation," she said.

"I certainly am glad to hear you say that," commented the principal's secretary, overhearing the conversation. "That was my house when I attended Brookline in 1936."

A study was made by the faculty at the Azusa, California, High School in 1961, aimed at analyzing the unit plan's degree of success after five years of operation. Results showed staff agreement that substantial progress in interpersonal relationships and in the exchange of ideas about operating the school had emerged from the plan. In addition, a cost analysis included in the study concluded that the unit plan did not increase staffing costs when compared with traditional school organization. Finally, the study found no significant defect inherent in the unit plan (36).

The following are reactions of students, taken from individual and group interviews in which students at Newton High School were asked to comment after one year's experience with little schools:

Now you go to an administrator who knows you when you are in difficulty rather than to a building supervisor who may never have seen you and is too busy to talk to you.

They know you now. You can't get away with as much as before so you don't try it. You know that ———— will be calling home.

Activity participation is much more important and is done more. We can win trophies for our house.

House dances are a flop. Very few attend.

There is more opportunity for participation in student activities and with it some individual recognition. The top jobs used to seem impossible to reach (35:133).

Cautious optimism typified the statements of school officials who reacted to schools within a school after using the plan for one year. They felt that the plan cannot be adequately judged until a class has had its entire high school experience with this form of organization. Yet the officials are optimistic about their experience and wish to explore further possibilities for the organization (24).

Problems and limitations

Problems faced when organizing schools within a school are similar to those in traditionally organized institutions. They include personnel, curriculum, and costs. Each of these will be discussed as related to little-school organization.

Personnel

Since the unit principal leads the little-school pupils and faculty, a well qualified person is vital. As the unit enrollment and staff increase, as the unit principal is given increasing responsibility in curriculum and guidance, his training and experience

68

must prepare him for a wider role. At Cleburne, Texas, where there are six schools within the school, the occasional inability to secure well-qualified unit principals was specifically cited as a weakness in the plan (35). In filling this position, Brookline's rotation plan bears further study.

Another personnel matter concerns maintaining balanced staff qualifications among the units. A similar problem confronts an administrator with more than one high school in the district. Reasonable staff balance is required or there will be requests to transfer to the better school. Although this could become a problem in decentralized schools, those who have used the organization have not named it as such. To prevent imbalance, one school rotates personnel each two years (23). Other administrators have felt, however, that the normal teacher turnover would enable them to maintain staff balance.

A faculty lacking sensitivity to the individual may limit the effectiveness of the little-school plan. Here lies the challenge for the school principals and their unit leaders: to keep teachers sensitive to their responsibility to the individual and to give them the working conditions, the environment, and the instructional tools to achieve good instruction for each child (16).

In schools within a school, however, a teacher's awareness of youth must extend beyond instruction. If the presumed advantage of better guidance is to become a reality, teachers must be willing to study youth as individuals. Morris reminds us that a genuine desire to know about youth and a willingness to accept facts about them are fundamental to fruitful study (29). As with instruction, then, a positive faculty attitude is essential.

Curriculum

Several matters that may limit extension of little schools involve the curriculum. How many subjects shall be offered exclusively in each unit? To what extent shall ability grouping affect placement in classes? Faculty decisions about these related

69

questions determine the unit's curricular role. For example, a school strongly given to ability grouping may assign all classes schoolwide to refine the groups to the greatest extent. Another faculty, given similar circumstances, would prefer to assign more classes within the little schools and limit ability grouping. The latter action seems more appropriate to building the continuing personal relationships basic to little-school philosophy.

Coordinate with the above are curriculum integration and the amount of emphasis subject-matter departments should receive in the school. While limited departmentalization is necessary in a large high school, emphasis on these subject-matter units has been a continuing concern of educators hoping to improve curriculum integration. Departmentalization, it can readily be seen, is at the opposite organizational pole from little-school organization, which emphasizes the student.

Austin, French, and Hull have outlined a solution to the student-subject quandary. They indicate that academic departments in most schools organize on a *process* basis, while vocational departments in these schools organize according to *purposes* to be achieved. Such diversity in basis of organization, the authors feel, splits the organization and weakens the structure. They therefore recommend that all elements of the school center on the school's purposes, with coordinators appointed to see that departments dovetail their work to achieve the purposes (5). Using this proposal with little-school organization, four little-school principals could be responsible for lifework education, leisure and recreational education, citizenship education, and health education—the major purposes suggested by Austin, French, and Hull.

Costs

Faculties must be cognizant of costs as they search for better ways to organize the high school. Many have decentralized to obtain the virtues of smallness with the economies of bigness.

While communities may save in construction costs by building central facilities for one large school rather than four smaller schools, little evidence exists about staffing costs for traditional schools compared with those organized on the little-school plan.

At Scarsdale, New York, however, it is felt that unit organization has not increased costs in the junior high school; it is thought that conventional organization could not reduce costs significantly (17). A study at Fairfield, Connecticut, showed that little-school costs would vary from less to slightly more than traditional organization, depending upon whether the housemasters and assistants taught one or two classes (43). Cost experience at Azusa High School was reported on page 67.

With the professional salary budget in many schools approximately 70 to 75 per cent of total current operating costs, obviously a change in the pupil-teacher, pupil-counselor, or pupil-administrator ratio will change total costs accordingly, under any plan of organization. Schools organized and staffed as little schools do not have to cost more. A traditionally organized institution might assign its assistant principal, guidance director, dean of girls, and dean of boys as unit administrators without changing costs. Yet if this school needs more administrative time, as most high schools do (5), assigning other faculty members as unit administrators will change the administrative ratio and increase costs.

A final word about costs relates to community understanding and school costs. Public schools are public business; school costs concern the taxpayers. While the public should be involved in the introduction of schools within a school, as seen in the next section, public understanding is particularly important where increased costs will result. Here, the school must clearly present alternatives as they affect the individual's development, as well as the consequences of choosing these alternatives. With alternatives specified, with the consequences clearly indicated, the setting for wise community choices is established (22).

ACTION

Examples described in this monograph, plus the institutions listed in the appendix, indicate that the schools-within-a-school plan is a tested form of organization. The ideas presented here are used today in America. Enough schools have the plan, and enough buildings are specifically designed for it, to give substantial direction to those interested.

The principal and staff planning a new building to house schools within a school should refer to other sources (4, 30) for general planning advice. For those moving to this plan in a new or old building, this section discusses five questions that should be considered for successful local action.

(1) Are you planning a new organization *and* a new building?

Most faculties adopting little-school organization in the last decade did so as a part of their planning for one or more new schools. While determining the educational program, they realized the need for new organization. The reader is urged to give as much thought to the organization as he does to the new building; an administrator's skill is thoroughly tested in introducing change into an organization acceptably and in orderly fashion (21).

(2) Are you following a sound pattern in organizing?

Thought and action about organization should follow a logical sequence. Griffiths *et al.* stress that the process of reorganizing or originally organizing a staff requires long hours of hard work and the chief school administrator's direction. They advocate the following nine minimum steps as guidelines:

1. The purposes of the school should be stated clearly and in operational terms.
2. The conceptual framework on which the organization will be constructed must be agreed upon.

72

3. The functions of administration necessary to the achievement of the stated purpose must be listed.
4. The present administrative structure must be surveyed to determine which functions are being performed by whom.
5. A plan of organization must be developed consistent with the conceptual framework of organization.
6. The functions of administration must be related to specific administrative positions.
7. Job descriptions must be developed for the administrative positions to which functions are assigned.
8. The administrative positions and the job descriptions must be related to the incumbent administrators (21:309).

(3) Are you involving others?

The participation of those affected in planning secondary schools is an accepted practice. Administrators planning decentralized schools and buildings to house them have used such participation in varying degrees. In Syosset, New York, the planning was largely done by the superintendent and professional consultants. A nine-member study committee, plus consultant and architectural help, planned Topeka West High School. At Newton, staff, students, parents, and lay citizens were involved.

It is highly recommended that there be broad staff and community participation in planning schools within a school. Unless the community conscience and concern are motivated to support the school's focus on the individual, staff planning will be ineffectual (22). York's study found that wide involvement was especially important in planning a substantial departure from the usual secondary school building (43). The article "A House Plan for Newton High School" (12) is an excellent description of total involvement in planning and orientation. It includes a list of sixteen questions raised by the Newton staff prior to decentralization.

(4) Are you allowing enough time?

Time is needed to plan and introduce a new organization in a new or old building. Involving others demands time. A basic rule of plant planning is "begin early!" It is listed here because of its extreme importance when considering a new organization *and* a new building.

(5) Are you trying the new organization in an existing building?

This excellent technique, not possible in all districts, has been used successfully in several communities. They began early to plan a new high school, decided to organize schools within the school, put the plan in operation in an existing institution, and then used decentralization in both when the new building was completed. White Plains, for example, had used little schools in its old building for seven years before moving into the new high school.

Since they were remaining in an older building, the Evanston staff used a variation of the above. A school within the school was operated on the third floor for two years while the remaining floors were under traditional administration. When the plan proved successful, it was adopted throughout the building.

SUMMARY

This chapter has sketched advantages to be gained, problems to be faced, and action to be considered in organizing schools within a school. In essence, then, it is the heart of the monograph for those wishing to know the plus and minus of little-school organization, and for those determined to begin.

CONCLUSION

The principal and his staff organize schools within a school to strengthen their focus on each individual and thus to improve the quality of education. They will succeed as they recognize the purposes of such organization, root their organization in sound principles, and periodically evaluate the structure to improve the plan. They will succeed as they are convinced their school can be improved.

A plan of organization will not guarantee improved education. Goodlad reminds us that no scheme of school organization, however elaborately worked out, provides for the types and ranges of learner variability encompassed by the school (22). Nevertheless, through schools within a school the principal and his staff can sharpen their focus on the individual.

Appendix

SCHOOLS REPORTED AS USING
SCHOOLS-WITHIN-A-SCHOOL ORGANIZATION

Location	School
1. Azusa, California	Azusa High School
2. Azusa, California	Citrus Union High School
3. Bellflower, California	Bellflower High School
4. Bellflower, California	Mayfair High School
5. Carmichael, California	San Juan Unified School District
6. Escondido, California	Escondido High School
7. Glendora, California	Glendora High School
8. San Diego, California	Samuel Gompers Junior High School
9. Fairfield, Connecticut	Andrew Warde High School
10. Fairfield, Connecticut	Roger Ludlow High School
11. Groton, Connecticut	Senior High School
12. Old Saybrook, Connecticut	Junior-Senior High School
13. Atlanta, Georgia	William A. Bass High School
14. Decatur, Georgia	Southwest Dekalb High School
15. Blue Island, Illinois	Blue Island High School
16. Des Plaines, Illinois	Maine West High School
17. Evanston, Illinois	Evanston Township High School
18. Glenview, Illinois	Glenbrook South High School
19. Joliet, Illinois	Joliet Township High School East
20. Joliet, Illinois	Joliet Township High School West
21. Skokie, Illinois	Niles North High School
22. Indianapolis, Indiana	North Central High School
23. Newton, Kansas	Newton Junior High School

77

Location	School
24. Topeka, Kansas	Eisenhower Junior High School
25. Topeka, Kansas	Jardine Junior High School
26. Topeka, Kansas	Topeka West High School
27. Baltimore, Maryland	Junior High School
28. Frederick, Maryland	Frederick County High School
29. Prince Frederick, Maryland	Calvert County High School
30. Washington County, Maryland	Boonsboro High School
31. Washington County, Maryland	Hancock High School
32. Washington County, Maryland	North Hagerstown High School
33. Washington County, Maryland	South Hagerstown High School
34. Brookline, Massachusetts	Brookline High School
35. Newton, Massachusetts	Newton High School
36. Newton, Massachusetts	Newton South High School
37. Detroit, Michigan	Eastern High School
38. Flint, Michigan	Longfellow Community Junior High School
39. Flint, Michigan	Bryant Community Junior High School
40. Flint, Michigan	Southwestern Community High School
41. Kalamazoo, Michigan	Loy Norrix High School
42. Madison Heights, Michigan	Lamphere Senior High School
43. Muskegon, Michigan	Muskegon High School
44. Royal Oak, Michigan	Clarence Kimball High School
45. Traverse City, Michigan	Traverse City High School
46. Edina, Minnesota	Edina-Morningside High School
47. Wayzata, Minnesota	Wayzata Senior High School
48. Riverview Gardens, Missouri	Riverview Gardens High School
49. Hampton, New Hampshire	Winnacunnet High School
50. Beacon, New York	Beacon High School
51. Ithaca, New York	Ithaca High School
52. Plainview, Long Island, New York	Plainview Junior High School
53. Massena, New York	Massena Junior-Senior High School
54. New York, New York	Forest Hills High School
55. Niskayuna, New York	Van Antwerp Junior High School
56. North Colonie, New York	North Colonie High School
57. Rochester, New York	Gates Chili Central School District

Location	School
58. Scarsdale, New York	Scarsdale Junior High School
59. Syosset, New York	Syosset High School
60. White Plains, New York	White Plains Senior High School
61. Charlotte, North Carolina	Ashley Park Junior High School
62. Charlotte, North Carolina	Garinger High School
63. Brecksville, Ohio	Brecksville High School
64. Cleveland Heights, Ohio	Heights High School
65. Kettering, Ohio	Fairmont High School
66. Newark, Ohio	Newark High School
67. Tulsa, Oklahoma	Woodrow Wilson Junior High School
68. Ardmore, Pennsylvania	Ardmore Junior High School
69. Ardmore, Pennsylvania	Lower Merion Junior High School
70. Fallsington, Pennsylvania	Pennsbury High School
71. Cayce, South Carolina	Cayce High School
72. Columbia, South Carolina	A. C. Flora High School
73. Williamston, South Carolina	Palmetto High School
74. Johnson City, Tennessee	Johnson City High School
75. Cleburne, Texas	Cleburne High School
76. San Angelo, Texas	San Angelo High School
77. Tyler, Texas	J. B. Moore Junior High School
78. Roanoke, Virginia	Patrick Henry High School
79. Roanoke, Virginia	William Fleming High School
80. Edmonds, Washington	Edmonds High School
81. Tacoma, Washington	Clover Park Schools
82. Tacoma, Washington	Mount Tahoma High School
83. Fond du Lac, Wisconsin	Goodrich High School

Bibliography

1. American Assembly. "Commission Report, Education." *The Report of the President's Commission on National Goals.* New York: Columbia University, November, 1960. Pp. 2, 3.
2. American Association of School Administrators. *The High School in a Changing World.* Thirty-sixth Yearbook. Washington, D.C.: American Association of School Administrators, 1960.
3. ————. *Planning America's School Buildings.* Report of the Association's School Building Commission. Washington, D.C.: American Association of School Administrators, 1960.
4. ————, and others. *Labels and Fingerprints.* Washington, D.C.: National Education Association [n.d.].
5. Austin, David B., Will French, and J. Dan Hull. *American High School Administration: Policy and Practice.* New York: Holt, Rinehart and Winston, 1962.
6. Brownell, John A. "The Claremont Teaching Team Program." Claremont, Calif.: Claremont Graduate School, 1961.
7. Caverly, Ernest R. "House Plan in a High School." *School Executive,* 79:54–55 (November, 1959).
8. Clinchy, Evans. *High Schools 1962.* Profiles of Significant Schools. New York: Educational Facilities Laboratories, December, 1961.
9. ————. *Newton South High School, Newton, Massachusetts.* Profiles of Significant Schools. New York: Educational Facilities Laboratories, February, 1960.
10. Conant, James B. *The American High School Today.* New York: McGraw-Hill Book Company, 1959.
11. "Construction Information." White Plains, N.Y.: White Plains High School, November 16, 1960 (mimeographed).
12. Creedon, Gertrude C. "A House Plan for Newton High School." *Educational Forum,* 24:397–404 (May, 1960).
13. Dworkin, Martin S., ed. *Dewey on Education.* Classics in Education No. 3. New York: Bureau of Publications, Teachers College, Columbia University, 1959.

14. Educational Facilities Laboratories. *The Cost of a Schoolhouse.* New York: Educational Facilities Laboratories, 1960.
15. Endicott, Frank S., Camilla M. Low, Van Miller, and C. W. Sanford. "Report of Homeroom Organization." Evanston, Ill.: Evanston Township High School, April 30, 1956 (mimeographed).
16. Engleman, Finis E. "Don't Lose the Individual." *The School Administrator,* 18:2 (March 15, 1961).
17. Fogg, Walter F. "Scarsdale's Plan is Flexible and Relaxed." *The Nation's Schools,* 67:66–68 (June, 1961).
18. "Functions of the Division, White Plains High School." White Plains, N.Y.: White Plains High School, October, 1959 (mimeographed).
19. Grambs, Jean D., and others. *The Junior High School We Need.* Washington, D.C.: Association for Supervision and Curriculum Development, 1961.
20. Griffiths, Daniel E. *Administrative Theory.* New York: Appleton-Century-Crofts, 1959.
21. ———, and others. *Organizing Schools for Effective Education.* Danville, Ill.: Interstate Printers and Publishers, 1962.
22. Henry, Nelson, B., ed. *Individualizing Instruction.* Sixty-first Yearbook of the National Society for the Study of Education. Chicago: University of Chicago Press, 1962.
23. Hodgson, John H. "The Schools Within a School Plan." Unpublished Doctor of Education project report, Teachers College, Columbia University, 1958.
24. "How to Make a Big School Little." *School Management,* 6:59, 63 (February, 1962).
25. McLure, William P. "Structure of Educational Government: As Viewed by the Educator." In *Government of Public Education for Adequate Policy Making.* Urbana, Ill.: University of Illinois, Bureau of Educational Research, 1960. P. 31.
26. McNassor, Donald. "New Designs for Civic Education in the High School." In Franklin Patterson, ed., *The Adolescent Citizen.* Glencoe, Ill.: The Free Press, 1960. Pp. 312–334.
27. Mitchum, Paul M. *The High School Principal and Staff Plan for Program Improvement.* New York: Bureau of Publications, Teachers College, Columbia University, 1958.
28. Morphet, Edgar L., Roe L. Johns, and Theodore L. Reller. *Educational Administration.* Englewood Cliffs, N.J.: Prentice-Hall, 1959.
29. Morris, Glyn. *The High School Principal and Staff Study Youth.* New York: Bureau of Publications, Teachers College, Columbia University, 1958.
30. National Council on Schoolhouse Construction. *Guide for Planning*

School Plants. Nashville, Tenn.: National Council on Schoolhouse Construction, 1958.

31. "The New High School." *Overview,* 3:33–48 (March, 1962).
32. "Newton 'House Plan' Overcomes Problems of Bigness." *Overview* 1:115 (January, 1960).
33. Office of Education, United States Department of Health, Education, and Welfare. *Public Secondary Schools.* Washington, D.C.: United States Government Printing Office, 1961.
34. Perkins, Lawrence B. "The Many Lives of Evanston Township High School." *American School Board Journal,* 141:24–28 (September, 1960).
35. Plath, Karl R. "The School Within a School: A Study of the Organization of Selected Senior High Schools, With Possible Applications for Evanston Township High School." Unpublished Doctor of Education project report, Teachers College, Columbia University, 1961.
36. Price, Nelson C. "An Evaluation of the 'School-Within-A-School' Plan of Secondary School Organization." Azusa, Calif.: Azusa Unified School District, February, 1962.
37. *The Pursuit of Excellence.* Special Studies Report V, Rockefeller Brothers Fund. Garden City, N.Y.: Doubleday & Company, 1958.
38. "The School-Within-A-School." Roanoke, Va.: Roanoke City Public Schools, June, 1961.
39. "School Within a School." *School Management,* 3:33–36 (August, 1959).
40. Scott, W. J. "Nine Schools Make One." *Bulletin* of the National Association of Secondary School Principals, 29:78–87 (April, 1945).
41. "The Shape of Things to Come: High School, 1960." *Know Your High School.* White Plains, N.Y.: White Plains High School, April, 1960.
42. Walton, John. *Administration and Policy-Making in Education.* Baltimore: The Johns Hopkins Press, 1959.
43. York, William J. "The Schools Within a School: A Study of Selected Secondary Schools Which Embody This Plan of Organization." Unpublished Doctor of Education project report, Teachers College, Columbia University, 1958.